WEATHER AND CLIMATE

CLIMATE CHANGE AND YOU

HOW CLIMATE CHANGE AFFECTS YOUR LIFE

by Emily Raij

CAPSTONE PRESS
a capstone imprint

Capstone Captivate is published by Capstone Press, an imprint of Capstone.
1710 Roe Crest Drive, North Mankato, Minnesota, 56003.
www.capstonepub.com

Library of Congress Cataloging-in-Publication Data is available on the Library of
Congress website.
ISBN: 978-1-5435-9157-6 (library binding)
ISBN: 978-1-4966-5779-4 (paperback)
ISBN: 978-1-5435-9162-0 (ebook pdf)

Summary: Describes how scientists study climate change, what current research
shows, and what people can do to reverse its effects.

Image Credits
Shutterstock: a katz, 21, Air Images, 25, ArtisticPhoto, 23, Erik Agar, 11, FloridaStock,
13, Hung Chung Chih, 18, Javier Garcia, 19, liaszio, 17, manaemedia, cover (bottom
right), Modxka, 24, neenawat khenyothaa, 9, New Africa, 5, Rawpixel.com, 26,
Rich Carey, 15, Sepp photography, cover, 1, stevemart, 14, stockphoto mania, 29,
VLADJ55, 7, wavebreakmedia, 27

Artistic elements: Shutterstock: ArtMari, Creative Stall, Flas100, gigi rosa, MaddyZ,
Paket, Rebellion Works, rudall30

Editorial Credits
Erika L. Shores, editor; Tracy McCabe, designer; Kelly Garvin, media researcher;
Kathy McColley, premedia specialist

Words in **bold** are in the glossary.

All internet sites appearing in back matter were available and accurate when this
book was sent to press.

Capstone thanks Laura M. Klein, M.S., Ph.D., for her expertise in reviewing
this book.

Printed and bound in the USA.
PA99

TABLE OF CONTENTS

CHAPTER 1

WHAT CAUSES CLIMATE CHANGE?

Today you splashed in puddles on the way to the bus stop. The day before you needed a hat and sunblock. It was hot and sunny. What changed? The weather!

Weather changes day to day and season to season. Weather includes wind, rain, and snow. It also includes temperature. Temperature tells us how hot or cold something is. The weather is what is happening in the **atmosphere** at a certain time and place.

We expect the weather to change. We can even plan for it. But what about when the **climate** changes? Climate is the average weather in a place over a longer period of time. Earth's climate has always been changing. But now it is becoming harder to predict and more dangerous.

When you know the weather will be rainy, you can grab an umbrella.

Scientists know people are causing climate change in a big way. People started burning coal, oil, and natural gas 200 years ago. These **fossil fuels** are taken out of the ground. Factories, homes, and cars burn them. This releases a gas called carbon dioxide. Burning forests to clear land for farms and buildings does too. Garbage rotting in landfills also releases carbon dioxide.

Scientists have been measuring the carbon dioxide put into the atmosphere. As the number of people in the world has grown, so has the amount of carbon dioxide. This causes hotter temperatures because carbon dioxide absorbs heat given off by the earth. The layer of carbon dioxide and other **greenhouse gases** is getting too thick. Heat cannot get out. This **global warming** is just one part of climate change. Hotter temperatures on land and in water are changing weather patterns around the world. Examples of these changes are some places are getting much less rain while others are getting more.

A power plant that burns coal puts carbon dioxide into the air.

FACT

The average world temperature has increased by about 1 degree Fahrenheit (0.5 degree Celsius) since the year 1900. This may not sound like a lot, but before 1900, a change of 1 degree took 10,000 years. Seventeen of the 18 warmest years have happened since 2001.

CHAPTER 2

HOW DOES CLIMATE CHANGE AFFECT US?

Climate change is causing more dangerous weather than in the past. This extreme weather includes strong storms such as hurricanes. It also includes floods, heat waves, and wildfires. Hotter temperatures cause more **droughts**. When land and plants get too dry, it is easier for fires to start. They burn down forests and homes.

Droughts and warmer weather can change the time of year that plants and crops grow. If food doesn't grow well or at all, some people will not have enough to eat. Farmers have to move to find land with available water.

Crops cannot grow when the weather is too hot and dry.

Living things are affected by hotter temperatures. Climate change is making winters shorter and warmer. Spring is starting earlier in the year. Plants may grow before the animals that eat them return north from their winter homes. When those animals do return, the plants are no longer in bloom. This leaves less food.

Some birds have started laying eggs and nesting earlier in the year. This happens because they sense the warmer weather. Then these birds are being born before the bugs they need to eat have hatched.

FACT

Scientists studied more than 4,000 different kinds of animals around the world. They found that more than half are moving to find better climates.

Birds that arrive too early in spring may have trouble finding food to eat.

Animals in colder climates are losing their homes and the food they eat as well. Higher temperatures are melting **glaciers**. These huge moving pieces of ice are home to tiny sea algae. Small sea animals called plankton eat the algae. Fish eat the plankton. Those fish are food for seals. Seals are food for polar bears. This food chain starts with tiny living things. But it involves many animals. If one food source goes away, many animals can go hungry. They may even die.

Melting glaciers also cause sea levels to rise. That changes ocean **currents**. These currents are the back and forth movement of water. Changing currents and warmer oceans are causing more extreme weather. More ocean water is **evaporating**. Hurricanes gain energy from evaporated water off the ocean. As a result, hurricanes last longer and are stronger.

Melting sea ice makes it hard for polar bears to find food.

DEADLY WATER

Storm surges can happen during hurricanes. They happen when huge waves of water push ashore. Stronger hurricanes and rising sea levels mean much bigger storm surges.

Oceans take in carbon dioxide and heat from the atmosphere. Wind makes waves in the water. These waves mix the carbon dioxide into the water more. Oceans cover most of the planet. But there is a limit to how much carbon dioxide and heat they can safely take in. More carbon dioxide in the ocean is causing the water to be **acidic.** This in turn breaks down the shells and skeletons of sea animals. Without their shells and skeletons, crabs, snails, and coral cannot protect themselves. Dying sea life hurts people who catch and sell seafood for a living too. They need a good fishing season to make money.

A sea snail's shell shows damage from acidic water.

Corals live in connected groups called reefs.
When they die, the whole reef is affected.

FACT

Animals without shells are having trouble as
well. More acidic water hurts their senses. It's
hard for clownfish to spot enemies. It makes
it hard for sharks to find food too.

Freshwater in lakes and rivers is hurt by a warming climate as well. Warming temperatures cause more **precipitation** to fall as rain instead of snow. This is very true in mountain areas. The snow on top of mountains used to melt and run downhill slowly. It made its way into rivers and lakes. It then could be stored and used in towns and on farms.

Rain flows much faster than melting snow. Rainwater cannot be saved as easily during spring and summer. More water is needed in those dry times. Some states in the United States such as California are already having water problems. If this keeps up, those states may have more droughts and wildfires.

A thunderstorm brings rain to a mountain range.

Smog is a mix of smoke and fog. This mix makes it hard to see and breathe. It is caused by chemicals from factories and cars being released into the air. It turns the air brown or gray. This **pollution** in the atmosphere not only adds to climate change, but it hurts people's health.

Some cities are greatly affected by pollution. Los Angeles and Mexico City are in low areas with mountains around them. These cities have a lot of smog. The smog gets trapped and the wind cannot carry it away.

In cities with thick smog, some people wear masks. The masks keep them from breathing in pollution.

Thick smog in Mexico City makes it hard to see its buildings.

CHAPTER 3

WHAT ARE GOVERNMENTS DOING ABOUT CLIMATE CHANGE?

Climate change affects every country in the world. What are world leaders doing to fight it? In 2016, almost 200 countries signed an agreement. They said they would work on placing a limit on the rise in world temperature. The goal is to keep the increase to 3.6 degrees Fahrenheit (2 degrees Celsius). They hope this will greatly lower the effects of climate change.

Countries are trying to lower how much pollution is put into the air. They need to do that without hurting how much food is made or how companies make money.

World leaders met in New York City in 2016 to work on slowing climate change and the problems it is causing.

China is working on climate change problems. This country burns half of the world's coal supply each year. More than one-fourth of the world's pollution starts in China. The good news? China is spending lots of money on making clean energy. This energy is from sources that can be used again. They don't pollute either. Solar and wind are two kinds of clean energy. Solar energy comes from the sun.

The United States is also working on clean energy programs. Many businesses are trying to lower the carbon dioxide they put into the air. Some are using solar or wind energy to power their factories. Others are shipping goods on trucks that use less fuel. Many businesses are trying to use less packaging in the items they make or ship. This lowers how much waste is made and the energy used to make the packaging.

Solar panels rise out of the water in Shanghai, China.
The panels collect sunlight to make energy.

CHAPTER 4
WHAT CAN YOU DO TO HELP?

Everyone can fight climate change. We add carbon dioxide to the air by what we buy and use. We can use more clean energy. Some people have solar panels on their roofs. Solar energy never runs out. Other people use electric cars. These cars do not burn gasoline. People also walk or bike instead of driving. This lowers the amount of carbon dioxide put into the air even more.

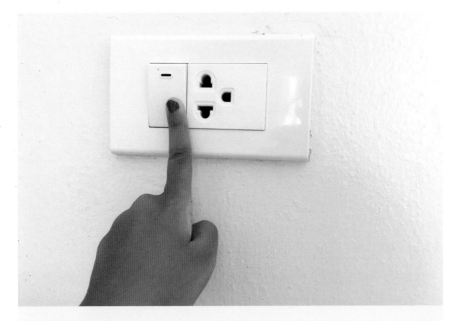

Save energy by turning off lights.

In homes, people can replace old washing machines, dryers, and dishwashers. New ones use less energy. People can turn off TVs, computers, and lights when not in use. People can also switch to light bulbs that last longer and need less energy.

Use new light bulbs that last longer.

Reduce, reuse, and recycle! These are good rules to follow. We can reduce the amount of waste we make. For example, we can avoid buying single-use items like paper plates and plastic forks. We can choose reusable items instead. That makes less waste for landfills. Use cloth shopping bags rather than plastic ones. Pack lunches in reusable containers instead of plastic bags. Don't buy bottled water. Take along a water bottle that can be used over and over. Of course, it's good to recycle too. Plastic, glass, and paper are kept out of landfills. They are then made into something else.

Recycling keeps more trash out of landfills.

A water bottle that can be washed and reused
is better for the planet.

COMPOST IT

Food and yard waste make up about one-third
of what people throw away. **Composting** mixes
rotting food and plants together. Then it is added to
soil to use in gardens. Composting keeps waste out
of landfills. This lessens the amount of harmful gas
put into the air as the food and plants rot.

People can change the way they eat and buy food. Eating less meat lowers how much harmful gas is put into the air by cows, pigs, and other livestock. Raising animals for their meat also uses a lot more energy and water than growing food in the ground.

Choosing food that is grown during the season you buy it also helps. Buy food that is grown nearby. It lowers pollution caused by bringing food in from faraway places. What's even better? Grow your own food in a backyard or town garden.

LOOKING TO THE FUTURE

Climate change is causing big problems. But we are always learning new ways to help the planet. People everywhere can work to slow down climate change and fix some of the problems it has caused.

Growing your own food goes a long way to help lower pollution.

GLOSSARY

acidic (A-suhd-ik)—containing acid; ocean water is made acidic by carbon dioxide mixing with it

atmosphere (AT-muhss-fihr)—the mixture of gases that surrounds Earth

climate (KLY-muht)—the average weather in a place over many years

compost (KOM-pohst)—to mix rotting food and plants together in order to reuse it to make soil richer

current (KUHR-uhnt)—the movement of water in a river or an ocean

drought (DROUT)—a long period of weather with little or no rainfall

evaporate (i-VA-puh-rayt)—process of change in water from a liquid to a gas

fossil fuels (FAH-suhl FYOOLZ)—formed from the remains of plants and animals; coal, oil, and natural gas are fossil fuels

glacier (GLAY-shur)—a large, slow-moving sheet of ice

global warming (GLOH-buhl WORM-ing)—rise in the average worldwide temperature of the atmosphere

greenhouse gas (GREEN-houss GAS)—gas in the atmosphere that traps heat energy; the greenhouse effect happens when certain gases in Earth's atmosphere absorb heat and make the air warmer

pollution (puh-LOO-shuhn)—harmful materials that damage the air, water, and soil

precipitation (pri-sip-i-TAY-shuhn)—water that falls from clouds to Earth

storm surge (STORM SURJ)—a huge wave of water pushed ashore by a hurricane

READ MORE

Biskup, Agnieszka. *Understanding Global Warming with Max Axiom Super Scientist*. North Mankato, MN: Capstone, 2019.

Haelle, Tara. *Turning Up the Heat*. Vero Beach, FL: Rourke Educational Media, 2019.

Labrecque, Ellen. *Climate Change*. Ann Arbor, MI: Cherry Lake Publishing, 2018.

INTERNET SITES

Climate Basics for Kids
https://www.c2es.org/content/climate-basics-for-kids/

Climate Change
https://kids.nationalgeographic.com/explore/science/climate-change/

Climate Kids
https://climatekids.nasa.gov/climate-change-meaning/

INDEX